Lerner SPORTS

SPORTS TEAM SMACKDOWN

NEW ENGLAND PATRIOTS VS. MIAMI DOLPHINS

RIVAL RUMBLE

ELLIOTT SMITH

Lerner Publications ◆ Minneapolis

Stats in this book are accurate through the 2024 NFL season.

Lerner Publications Company
An imprint of Lerner Publishing Group, Inc.
241 First Avenue North
Minneapolis, MN 55401 USA

For reading levels and more information, look up this title at www.lernerbooks.com.

Main body text set in Aptifer Sans LT Pro.
Typeface provided by Linotype AG.

Editor: Matt Doeden
Lerner team: Martha Kranes

Library of Congress Cataloging-in-Publication Data

Names: Smith, Elliott, author.
Title: New England Patriots vs. Miami Dolphins : rival rumble / Elliott Smith.
Description: Minneapolis, MN : Lerner Publications, [2026] | Series: Sports team smackdown (Lerner sports) | Includes bibliographical references and index. | Audience: Ages 7–11 | Audience: Grades 4–6 | Summary: "From 2002 to 2019, the New England Patriots won six Super Bowls. The division-rival Miami Dolphins have won two Super Bowls and have a longer history of success. Which team wins this rival rumble?"— Provided by publisher.
Identifiers: LCCN 2024047106 (print) | LCCN 2024047107 (ebook) | ISBN 9798765668658 (library binding) | ISBN 9798765683514 (paperback) | ISBN 9798765681657 (epub)
Subjects: LCSH: New England Patriots (Football team)—Juvenile literature. | Miami Dolphins (Football team)—Juvenile literature. | Sports rivalries—Juvenile literature.
Classification: LCC GV956.N36 S65 2026 (print) | LCC GV956.N36 (ebook) | DDC 796.332092 [B]—dc23/eng/20250208

LC record available at https://lccn.loc.gov/2024047106
LC ebook record available at https://lccn.loc.gov/2024047107

Manufactured in the United States of America
1-1011975-53833-3/12/2025

TABLE OF CONTENTS

INTRODUCTION

MIAMI MIRACLE

The Miami Dolphins were in trouble. Just seven seconds remained in their December 2018 game with their rivals, the New England Patriots. Miami trailed 33–28 and was 69 yards away from the end zone. A win would give the Patriots their tenth straight American Football Conference (AFC) East division title. The Dolphins appeared to be headed to another tough loss.

Miami quarterback Ryan Tannehill took the snap and fired a 14-yard pass over the middle to wide receiver Kenny Stills. Stills tossed a lateral to wide receiver DeVante Parker. Parker

Patriots running back Sony Michel tries to avoid Dolphins tacklers as the teams clash in December 2018.

quickly lateraled the ball to running back Kenyan Drake near the 50-yard line.

Drake had a perfect angle along the sideline and great blocks from his teammates. As the Patriots chased Drake, only one man stood between him and a score. New England had put star tight end Rob Gronkowski in the game to defend against a long pass. But Gronkowski was no match for Drake's speed. Drake stormed past him into the end zone, where he threw the ball high into the stands in celebration. Miami had pulled off a stunning 34–33 win!

FAST FACTS

- Miami is the only NFL team to complete a perfect season, going 17-0 in 1972. The Patriots had an undefeated regular season in 2007 but lost in the Super Bowl.
- New England is tied with the Pittsburgh Steelers for most Super Bowl victories at six.
- Former Dolphins coach Don Shula leads the NFL in all-time coaching victories. Former Patriots coach Bill Belichick is second.
- New England quarterback Tom Brady's seven Super Bowl wins are the most by any player in NFL history.

It was the first time in National Football League (NFL) history that a game-winning touchdown was scored with multiple lateral passes. Fans called the play the Miami Miracle. It was another memorable moment between these longtime rivals. The Dolphins hold the slight edge in the all-time series, but the Patriots are one of the NFL's most successful teams. Which team is the best? Let the rival rumble begin!

Miami's Kenyan Drake sprints to the end zone with the ball.

SMACKDOWN!

CHAPTER 1

Defensive end Tony Sardisco (center left) *makes a tackle for the Boston Patriots in 1960.*

FROM AFL TO NFL

The Patriots formed in 1960 as the Boston Patriots. They were one of the original members of the American Football League (AFL). Team owners formed this league in 1960 to compete with the NFL. They started teams in cities without pro football. The Patriots played in several stadiums in the area during their time in the AFL, including Fenway Park where the Boston Red Sox play.

In 1963, the Patriots won their first and only AFL playoff game. When the AFL and NFL merged in 1970, the Patriots were placed in the AFC. They wanted to rename themselves the Bay State Patriots, but the NFL rejected the name. The New England Patriots, the team's second choice for a name, were born.

Patriots running back Billy Lott (right) fights for yards in a 1961 game against the Oakland Raiders.

At first, the Patriots only found mild success in the newly expanded NFL. Their only Super Bowl appearance was in 1986 when they lost to the Chicago Bears. New England's fortunes changed after the team hired Bill Belichick in January 2000. The same year, they drafted Tom Brady.

With Brady and Belichick, the Patriots became an NFL dynasty. They went to nine Super Bowls, winning six. The Patriots are tied with the Pittsburgh Steelers for most Super Bowl victories.

The Patriots made the Super Bowl after the 1985 season, but they couldn't beat the powerful Chicago Bears.

Patriots head coach Bill Belichick (left) shakes hands with team owner Robert Kraft in 2002.

The Miami Dolphins started in the AFL in 1966. By the time they joined the NFL in 1970, the Dolphins had one of football's best rosters. They were the first team to appear in

CHECK IT OUT

In 2007, the Patriots became the first NFL team to own their own planes for traveling to road games. The team bought two Boeing 767s!

Dolphins quarterback Earl Morrall throws a pass in the team's perfect 1972 season.

three straight Super Bowls. Miami lost to the Dallas Cowboys in 1972. Then the Dolphins won back-to-back Super Bowls in 1973 and 1974.

The 1972 team is the only NFL team to finish the season with an undefeated record. The Dolphins were a perfect 17–0 and won the Super Bowl in January 1973. Since then, Dolphins players from that team celebrate together when the last undefeated team in the league loses.

In the 1980s, quarterback Dan Marino led a high-powered Dolphins offense. While Miami regularly made the playoffs, they lost both of their trips to the Super Bowl. The Dolphins have not reached the big game since 1985.

The Patriots and Dolphins battle twice each year in the AFC East. Fans of both teams want to claim bragging rights. That makes every game an all-out showdown!

Dolphins quarterback Dan Marino searches for an open receiver in this 1984 game against the San Diego Chargers.

CHAPTER 2

Miami receiver Mark Ingram catches a touchdown pass after Dan Marino's famous fake spike.

AMAZING ACHIEVEMENTS

In 1994, the Dolphins trailed the New York Jets with less than a minute left in the fourth quarter. After quarterback Dan Marino completed a pass near the end zone, he hurried to run another play. He signaled that he would spike the ball to stop the clock.

When he took the snap, Marino didn't spike the ball. Instead, he took advantage of a relaxed Jets defense and fired a touchdown pass to Mark Ingram. The fake spike gave Miami a stunning 28–24 victory.

Miami completed one of the coolest trick plays in the 2019 season. Trailing the Philadelphia Eagles 13–7, the Dolphins sent kicker Jason Sanders and punter Matt Haack onto the field. Instead of kicking a short field goal, Haack lined up as quarterback. When the play started, he tossed the ball to a wide-open Sanders in the end zone for a touchdown. It was the first time in NFL history that a punter had thrown a touchdown pass to a kicker.

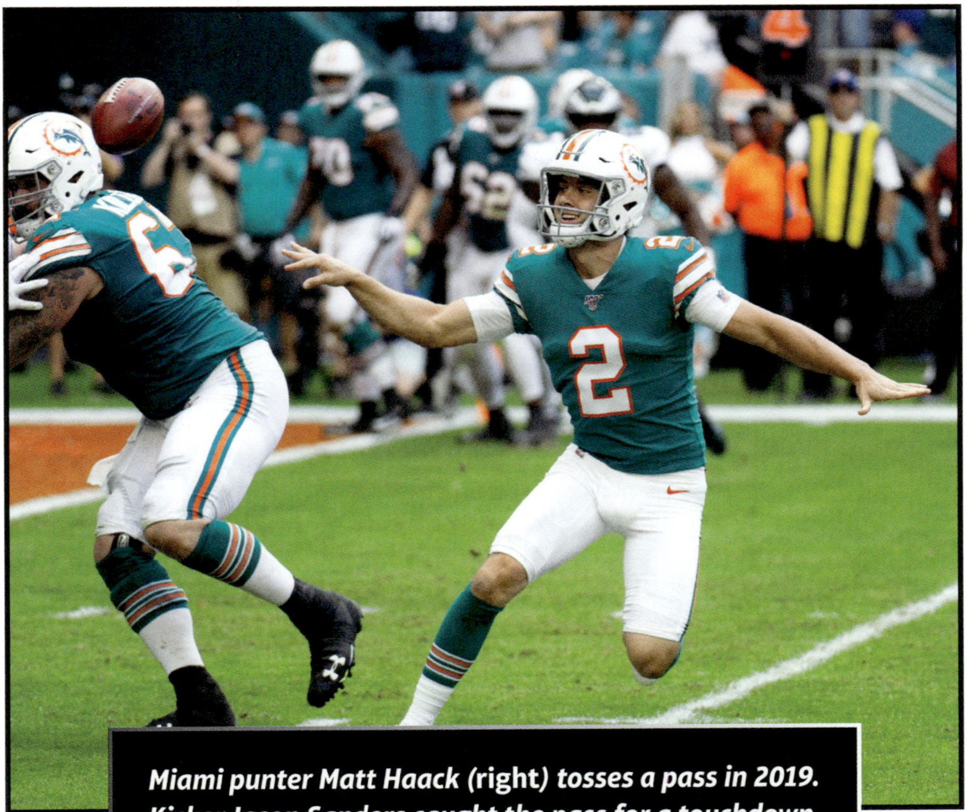

Miami punter Matt Haack (right) tosses a pass in 2019. Kicker Jason Sanders caught the pass for a touchdown.

Mud-covered linebacker A. J. Duhe celebrates a touchdown for Miami in the 1982 AFC Championship Game.

Dolphins linebacker A. J. Duhe had an amazing day in the 1982 AFC Championship Game. He snagged three interceptions and ran one of them back for a touchdown. Miami's 14–0 victory sent the Dolphins to the Super Bowl.

Adam Vinatieri made many important kicks during his Patriots career. Two of his biggest occurred on a snowy night during the 2001 playoffs. With several inches of snow on the ground and more falling, Vinatieri made a 45-yard field goal to force overtime. Then he kicked a 23-yard field goal to give the Patriots a dramatic win over the Oakland Raiders.

The Patriots have a history of huge Super Bowl moments. None was bigger than what happened in the final seconds of the 2015 Super Bowl. The Seattle Seahawks were on the 1-yard line and needed a touchdown to win.

Most fans thought that the Seahawks would call for a run play. But New England cornerback Malcolm Butler expected a pass. Butler jumped in front of the Seattle receiver when quarterback Russell Wilson fired a pass. Butler's shocking interception sealed another New England Super Bowl victory.

Patriots safety Malcolm Butler intercepts a pass in the final seconds to seal the Super Bowl win for the Patriots.

Quarterback Tom Brady throws a pass in the 2017 Super Bowl against the Falcons.

The 2017 Super Bowl was one of the most exciting games in NFL history. The Patriots trailed the Atlanta Falcons 28–3. But New England mounted a furious fourth quarter comeback. With 2:28 left in the game, Tom Brady fired a pass toward receiver Julian Edelman. An Atlanta defender tipped the pass. The ball spun in the air. Three Falcons defenders

CHECK IT OUT

On September 24, 2023, the Dolphins beat the Denver Broncos 70–20! Miami's 70 points were the most scored by an NFL team since 1966.

tried to catch it. But Edelman somehow came away with it. The catch kept the drive alive. New England went on to win in overtime.

Tom Brady (right) celebrates his team's big comeback win in the Super Bowl with teammates Julian Edelman (center) and David Andrews (left).

CHAPTER 3

Cornerback Ty Law leaps for an interception in 2002.

LEGENDS AND LEADERS

The Patriots have 11 members in the Pro Football Hall of Fame. They will certainly have more in the future. New England's dynasty of the 2000s had stars on every part of the field.

Defensive standouts Ty Law, Richard Seymour, and Andre Tippett are among the New England greats in the Hall of Fame. Offensive players such as John Hannah and Ben Coates were superstars. Young standouts such as Christian Gonzalez and Drake Maye are part of New England's future.

Many experts call Tom Brady the greatest quarterback of all time. He leads the NFL record books in most passing stats, including passing yards and regular-season wins. He also has seven Super Bowl wins, the most of any player.

Rookie quarterback Drake Maye (left) escapes a defender in this 2024 game against the Dolphins.

Legendary coach Bill Belichick roamed the sidelines in New England for 24 seasons. He was the mastermind of the Patriots dynasty. Belichick ranks second all-time in coaching victories.

Miami has its own coaching legend. Don Shula leads the NFL in all-time wins after coaching the Dolphins for 26 seasons. He is one of 18 Dolphins in the Hall of Fame.

Head coach Don Shula (left) with quarterbacks Earl Morrall (right) and Bob Griese (center) in December 1972

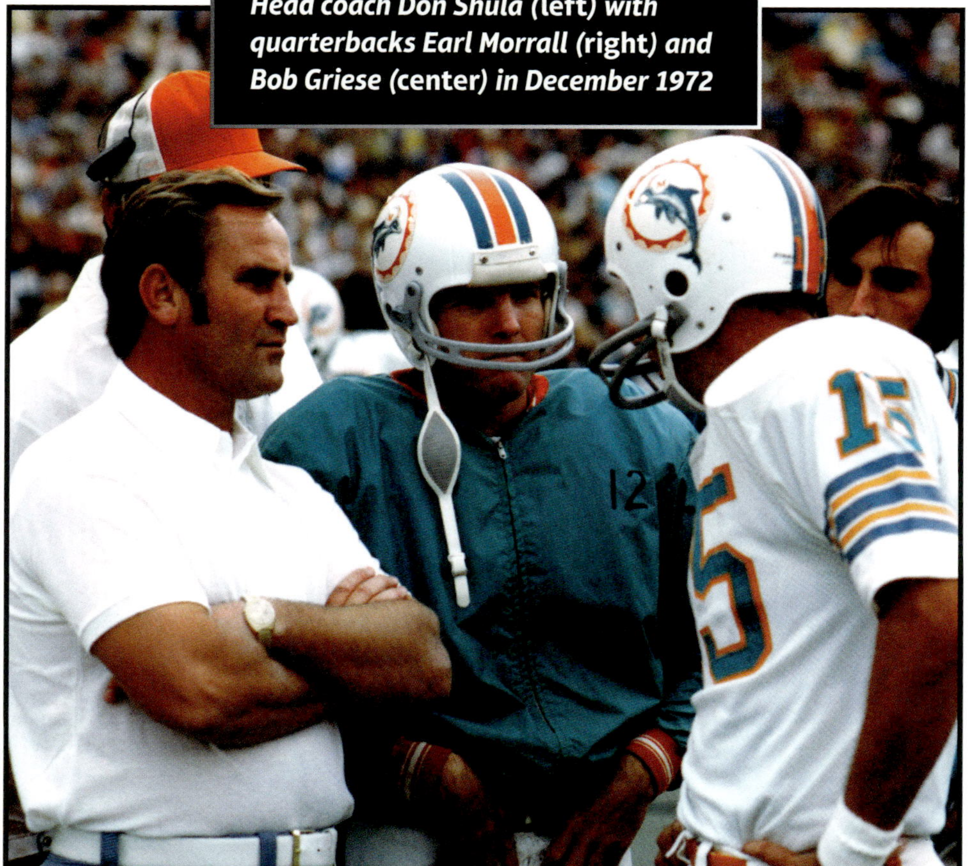

Wide receiver Tyreek Hill tries to avoid a tackle in this 2024 game against the Jets.

Quarterback Dan Marino was the face of the Dolphins for many years. He finished his career with 420 touchdown passes. Other offensive standouts include running back Larry Csonka and wide receiver Paul Warfield. On defense, defensive end Jason Taylor and linebacker Zach Thomas helped shut down opposing offenses.

Modern Dolphins look to restore the team to its previous glory. Receivers Tyreek Hill and Jaylen Waddle form one

CHECK IT OUT

From 2000 to 2023, the Patriots had the most wins in the NFL with 267. The Dolphins ranked 17th with 189.

of the NFL's fastest duos. Quarterback Tua Tagovailoa has battled injuries in his career. But when healthy, he makes the Dolphins a threat to score every time they touch the ball.

Hall of Fame linebacker Nick Buoniconti was a star player for both teams. He started his career with the Patriots and then won two Super Bowls with the Dolphins.

Quarterback Tua Tagovailoa (center) waits for the snap in this 2024 game against the Houston Texans.

CHAPTER 4

Dolphins defender Zach Sieler sacks quarterback Drake Maye in 2024.

CHOOSE YOUR CHAMPION

It's fun debating which team is the best. No choice is right or wrong. There are arguments to be made for fans of both teams!

The Dolphins are the only team to ever complete an undefeated season. They have two Super Bowl wins. And Miami has always featured some of the best offensive players in the league.

The Patriots have six Super Bowl wins in their trophy case. Tom Brady may have been the greatest quarterback of all time. And New England is one of the most popular teams in the US.

Wide receiver Jaylen Waddle (center) celebrates with tight end Jonnu Smith (right) after a Dolphins touchdown.

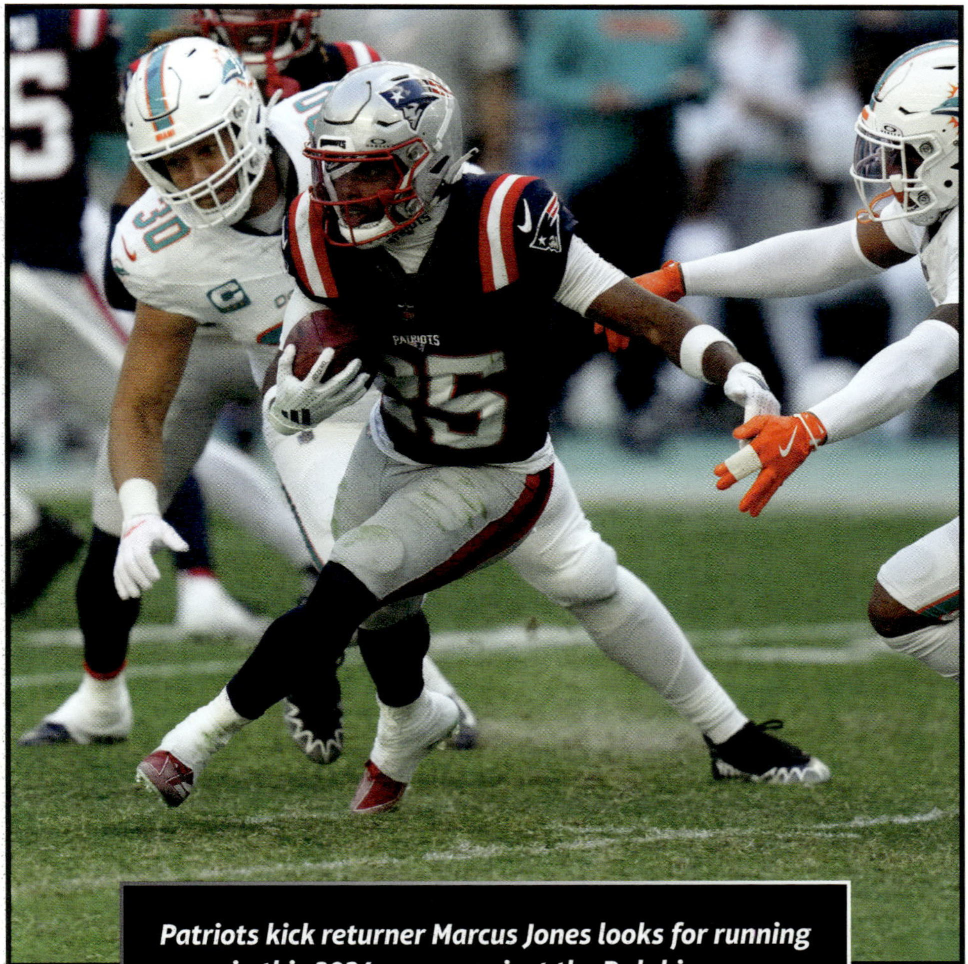

Patriots kick returner Marcus Jones looks for running room in this 2024 game against the Dolphins.

In this showdown between AFC East rivals, the Dolphins hold the upper hand in their head-to-head matchups. But it's hard to ignore the Patriots' dynasty. Therefore, the edge goes to New England!

Now it's your turn. Who do you think wins this football smackdown?

SMACKDOWN TIMELINE

MIAMI DOLPHINS

1966 The Miami Dolphins form as part of the American Football League.

1970 The Dolphins join the NFL.

1972 The Dolphins become the only NFL team to go undefeated in the regular season and playoffs.

1973 Miami wins its second straight Super Bowl.

1983 The Dolphins select quarterback Dan Marino with the 27th pick in the NFL Draft.

1987 The team moves into Hard Rock Stadium after 21 seasons in the Orange Bowl.

1993 Don Shula breaks the NFL's all-time coaching wins record.

2023 The Dolphins score 70 points in a win over Denver, the most scored by a team since 1966.

NEW ENGLAND PATRIOTS

1960 The Boston Patriots become an original member of the American Football League.

1970 The Patriots join the NFL and are renamed the New England Patriots.

2000 The Patriots hire Bill Belichick as head coach.

2002 New England wins its first Super Bowl.

2007 The Patriots finish the regular season undefeated but lose in the Super Bowl.

2016 New England trails Atlanta 28–3 in the Super Bowl before coming back to win 34–28.

2018 The Patriots beat the Los Angeles Rams for their sixth Super Bowl title.

2023 Bill Belichick leaves the Patriots after 24 seasons with the team.

2025 The team hires Mike Vrabel as head coach.

GLOSSARY

cornerback: a defensive player whose main job is to prevent completed passes

division: a group of teams that directly compete against one another

dynasty: a team that wins multiple championships during a short time

end zone: the area on a football field where touchdowns are scored

interception: when a pass is caught by the defense

lateral: a sideways or backward pass

linebacker: a defensive player who usually plays in the middle of the field

rivalry: when a player or team tries to defeat or be more successful than another

roster: a list of players on a team

snap: when the football is put in play by quickly passing it between the legs to a teammate

spike: when the quarterback throws the ball to the ground to stop the clock

LEARN MORE

Flynn, Brendan. *Miami Dolphins*. Mendota Heights, MN: North Star Editions, 2024.

Gigliotti, Jim. *Joe Burrow vs. Dan Marino: Who Would Win?* Minneapolis: Lerner Publications, 2025.

NFL Facts for Kids
https://kids.kiddle.co/National_Football_League

Pro Football Hall of Fame
https://www.profootballhof.com

Scheff, Matt. *New England Patriots*. Mendota Heights, MN: North Star Editions, 2025.

Sports Illustrated Kids: Football
https://www.sikids.com/football

INDEX

PHOTO ACKNOWLEDGMENTS

Image credits: AP Photo/Logan Bowles, p. 4; AP Photo/David Santiago/*Miami Herald*, p. 6; AP Photo/Greg M. Cooper, p. 7 (top); AP Photo/Doug Murray, p. 7 (bottom); AP Photo/Bob Campbell/*San Francisco Chronicle*, pp. 8, 9; AP Photo/Lennox McLendon, p. 10; AP Photo/Steven Senne, p. 11; AP Photo, p. 12; AP Photo/Paul Spinelli, p. 13; John Iacono/*Sports Illustrated*/Getty Images, p. 14; Doug Murray/Icon Sportswire/Getty Images, p. 15; AP Photo/Al Messerschmidt, p. 16; AP Photo/Matt Rourke, p. 17; Gregory Shamus/Getty Images, pp. 18, 19; AP Photo/Allen Kee, p. 20; AP Photo/Miami Dolphins, pp. 21, 23, 25, 26; Ross Lewis/Getty Images, p. 22; AP Photo/Eric Christian Smith, p. 24; AP Photo/Lynne Sladky, p. 27. Design element: Trisno Wardana/Shutterstock; Ihor Biliavskyi/Shutterstock; Joko Ribowo/Shutterstock.

Cover: AP Photo/Michael Owens; AP Photo/Miami Dolphins.